And to think that I saw it on K Street N.W.

Written & illustrated
by Dr. Susie

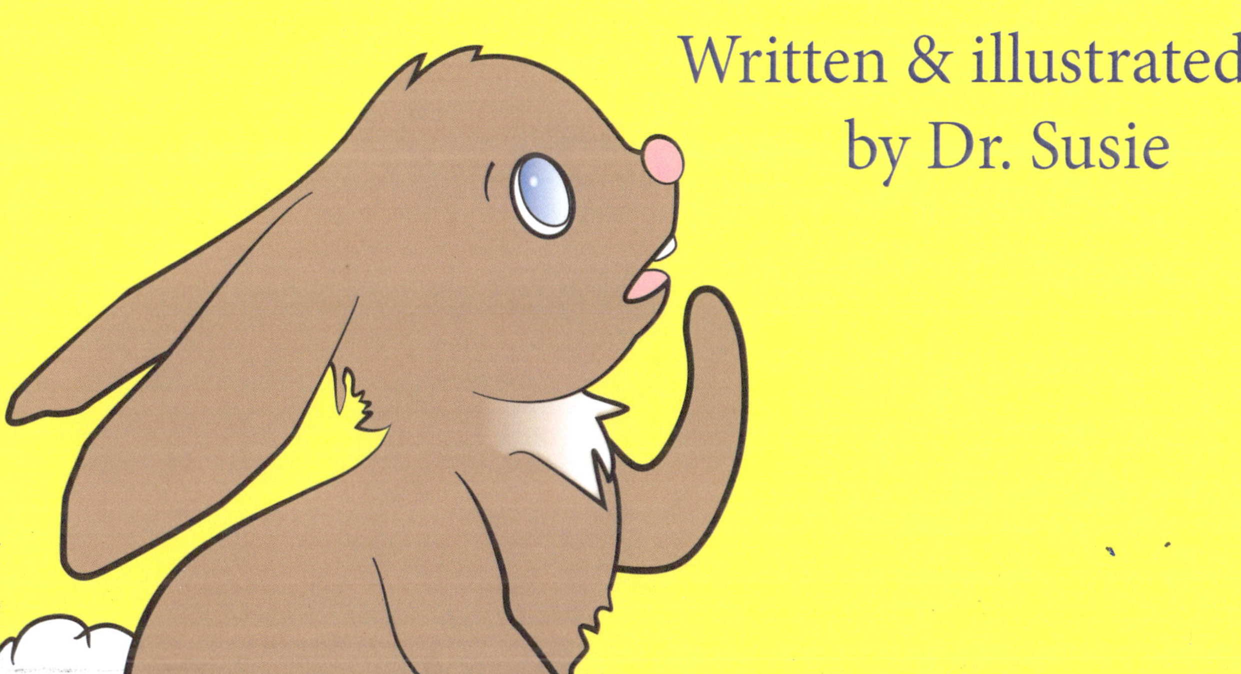

for Alfie

Three weeks ago Thursday at 2:33

I took myself over to K Street D.C.

It's a place, I had heard, with the best congregation

Of fabulous lobbying firms in the nation.

I wanted to see with my very own eyes

If the hype were all true, or a pack full of lies.

So I said to myself, "Don't hold back! Sally forth!"

And I hopped on the Metro to Farragut North.

5

It didn't take long for the train to arrive.

In fact, it was just about 2:35.

And as I emerged from the rail to the street,

A lump formed in my throat, and my heart

skipped a beat.

Could I really be here? Would it be like they said?

Oodles of dough, and mountains of bread?

The center of D.C.'s political power?

A modern-day high roller's ivory tower?

The sun shone down brightly, and it made me blink.

I was blind for a moment, but oh! what a stink!

And what was that sound now assaulting my ear?

A high-pitched discordance that filled me with fear.

As the scene came in view, (what a stroke of bad luck!)

There were millions of piglets all running amok,

Oinking and grunting and squeaking and squealing,

The terrible shock of the sight left me reeling.

There were big ones and small ones,

some sized in the middle,

There were slim ones and fat ones, and some going piddle.

"This place is a pig sty!" I said right out loud,

When a voice from behind me called,

"My, aren't we proud?"

I spun on my heel to find out who was there.
This chap had a cane and pomade in his hair,
With a big toothy grin and cheeks red as a fruit,
A D.C. fat cat in a large three-piece suit.

"You're new to the neighborhood, aren't you, young sir?"
When I said that I was, he then started to purr.
"Welcome to K Street, where we raise the pork,
As important a spot as Wall Street to New York!

"Here's where the rich come to slop all the hogs.
When they get big enough, we toss them to the dogs
Up on Capitol Hill, where like so many kings,
They add them to bills that have lots of purse strings."

CO₂

He said what he does is snoop, mix, pry and meddle
And gets paid the big bucks to influence peddle.
"I plan covert bribes, make an art of deceit,
To fleece the taxpayer and serve the elite."

Each piglet, he said, was a project or scheme,
Intended to bolster the current regime.
"This one, case in point," (as he scooped up a swine)
"Will someday become a pet project design."

There were piglets for windmills and flat solar cells
And bridges to nowhere and deep carbon wells,
Museums about things that don't really matter,
And welfare payouts to make fat people fatter.

Some would grow into cash for a prized interest perk
Or funding to study how useless things work.
There'd be money to save an endangered crustacean
With plenty left over for trade regulation.

"When they're through on the Hill,

pols come here - call it karma -

To lobby for Big Tech, Big Finance, Big Pharma,

To make sure redundancies prosper and thrive,

While gathering salaries on overdrive."

BIG
Finance
$
!!!

I was taken aback by this bloated furball,

So full of foul hubris and hot air and gall.

And while dodging a piglet, I said to the creep,

"How can you live with yourself? Can you sleep?"

He twirled his long cane, and he chuckled with glee.

"Son, without K Street, now where would you be?

No Congressman knows his right hand from his left,

So we're there to guide him and manage the theft.

"We're brilliant and sly; though we've earned ill-repute,

When it comes to your taxes, there's no substitute.

Who else knows just how to spend money so well?"

And he strode down 14th toward the Willard Hotel."

It was from that direction I noticed just then
A flurry of waddle-ing, squawking young men
Tottering toward me, right past that last fellow,
A gaggle of journalists all dressed in yellow!

Behind them in rows, and with eyes half asleep,
Filed a flock of subservient, freshly-fleeced sheep.
And as the hacks rattled off scads of fake news,
Their followers trudged - both the rams and the ewes.

"Dateline, K Street," one reporter began.
"Where locals work hard for the plain, common man.
They're expert technicians with flawless insight
And rare sympathy for the working man's plight."

"They identify matters of public malfeasance,
Petition the Hill for a redress of grievance,
Then write complex bills on which you can rely
To skillfully turn any Congressman's 'aye.'"

The news team went on praising lobby connections

Theoretically used to make legal corrections.

And as they continued their puff and patois,

The sheep chewed their cud and droned, "Baa, baa, baa, baa."

"They're not here for those reasons," I just had to say.

"Did you see that fat cat that you passed on your way?

He told me that he buys political favors,

Like tax breaks and aid grants and agency waivers!"

"I've fact-checked your statement," honked one of the crew.

"It's hateful to those classed LGBTQ!

Plus, there's the point you cannot guarantee:

How do you know that his pronoun is he?"

"I've fact-checked you, too!" broke in one ruffled bird.
(He was one of the very most fowl of the herd.)
"You're racist and sexist and homotransphobic,
Conspiracy theorist, deranged paranoiac!"

"No, no, that's not right!" I cried, shaking my head.
"You must print retractions, report truth instead!"
But they squawked even louder of disinformation,
Election denial and polarization.

I raised my voice higher: "If all that is true,
Then say why this place is a rank porcine zoo."
"That's hate speech!" honked one,
as another chimed in,
"The pigs migrated here
'cause of global warmin'!"

"It's your carbon footprint that clarifies why
The hogs lost their biome and might even die.
It's also the reason these poor sheep are bald,"
He said, and then finished with, "Humph! I'm appalled!"

I turned to the sheep. "Pay no heed to these geese.
It's the lobbyists' fault that you've lost all your fleece."
But it was too late. They weren't listening to me.
In fact, they were frowning quite menacingly.

A tall gander hissed, "Now just look what you've done!

You've upset them!" And that's when I started to run,

Because close on my heels was a massive stampede

Bleating threats, throwing bricks and pursuing with speed.

In my haste to get out of this K-Street kerfuffle,

I tripped on a pink piglet eating a truffle,

Which angered the hogs, who joined in on the riot

And added their squeals to the ovine disquiet.

You can never imagine the trouble I faced

As the crazed herds advanced and insulted and chased.

But just as I thought, "This is hopeless! I'm through!"

I jumped on a last-minute Metro choo-choo.

Now, you'd think this is where my sad story would end,

But sorry to say, there's more to it, my friend,

For headlining on the next day's front-page news

Was: "K Street Invaded by Local Yahoos."

They said I had led a domestic insurgence

And warned of a possible coming resurgence

And issued a shelter-in-place until clear,

While animal protests went on in high gear.

And now I'm suspended on YouTube and Facebook.

I made FBI's list as most-wanted hate crook.

All 'cause I unearthed a huge hornets' nest,

And to think that I saw it on K Street NW.

The End